*Memory and Consciousness*

By Annie Besant
Helena P. Blavatsky

Copyright © 2021 Lamp of Trismegistus. All rights reserved. No part of this publication may be reproduced or transmitted in any form or by any means, electronic or mechanical, including photocopying, recording, or by any information storage and retrieval system, without permission in writing from Lamp of Trismegistus. Reviewers may quote brief passages.

ISBN: 978-1-63118-582-3

*Esoteric Classics*

## Other Books in this Series and Related Titles

*Aurora of the Philosophers* by Paracelsus (978-1-63118-507-6)

*Clairvoyance and Psychic Abilities* by A Besant &c (978-1-63118-403-1)

*The Feminine Occult* by various authors (978-1-63118-711-7)

*Rosicrucian Rules, Secret Signs, Codes and Symbols* by various (978-1-63118-488-8)

*An Outline of Theosophy* by C W Leadbeater (978-1-63118-452-9)

*Paracelsus, the Four Elements and Their Spirits* by M P Hall (978-1-63118-400-0)

*Essays on Ancient Magic* by Helena P Blavatsky (978-1-63118-535-9)

*Essays on the Esoteric Tradition of Karma* by A Besant &c (978-1-63118-426-0)

*The Use of Evil* by Annie Besant (978-1-63118-532-8)

*The Alchemical Catechism of Paracelsus* by Paracelsus (978-1-63118-513-7)

*Alchemy in the Nineteenth Century* by Helena P Blavatsky (978-1-63118-446-8)

*Qabbalistic Teachings and the Tree of Life* by M P Hall (978-1-63118-482-6)

*The Historic, Mythic and Mystic Christ* by Annie Besant (978–1–63118–533–5)

*The Hidden Mysteries of Christianity* by Annie Besant (978–1–63118–534–2)

*History, Analysis and Secret Tradition of the Tarot* by Hall &c (978-1-63118-445-1)

*Crystal Vision Through Crystal Gazing* by Frater Achad (978-1-63118-455-0)

*The Golden Verses of Pythagoras: Five Translations* (978-1-63118-479-6)

*Arcane Formulas or Mental Alchemy* by W W Atkinson (978-1-63118-459-8)

*The Machinery of the Mind* by Dion Fortune (978-1-63118-451-2)

*The A E Waite Reader: A Selection of Occult Essays* (978-1-63118-515-1)

*The Leadbeater Reader: A Selection of Occult Essays* (978-1-63118-483-3)

**Audio versions are also available on Audible, Amazon and Apple**

**Other Books in this Series and Related Titles**

*The Origin of Evil* by Helena P Blavatsky (978–1–63118–581–6)

*The Camp of Philosophy: Studies in Alchemy* by Bloomfield (978–1–63118–580–9)

*The Testaments of the Twelve Patriarchs* (978–1–63118–579–3)

*Occult or Exact Science?* by Helena P Blavatsky (978–1–63118–578–6)

*Occultism, Semi-Occultism & Pseudo Occultism* by A Besant (978–1–63118–577–9)

*The Fourth-Gospel and Synoptical Problem* by G R S Mead (978–1–63118–576–2)

*On the Bhagavad-Gita* by T Subba Row &c (978–1–63118–575–5)

*What Theosophy Does for Us* by C W Leadbeater (978–1–63118–574–8)

*Spiritual Life for Man* by Annie Besant (978–1–63118–573–1)

*The Mysteries* by Annie Besant (978–1–63118–572–4)

*Fundamental Ideas of Theosophy* by Bhagwan Das (978–1–63118–571–7)

*Dreams: What They Are and Caused* by C W Leadbeater (978–1–63118–570–0)

*Communication Between Different Worlds* by Annie Besant (978–1–63118–569–4)

*Animism, Magic and the Omnipotence of Thought* by S Freud (978–1–63118–568–7)

*Buddhism* by F Otto Schrader (978–1–63118–567–0)

*Death* by W W Westcott (978–1–63118–566–3)

*The Religion of Theosophy* by Bhagwan Das (978–1–63118–565–6)

*The Spirit of Zoroastrianism* by Henry S Olcott (978–1–63118–564–9)

*The Brotherhood of Religions* by Annie Besant (978–1–63118–563–2)

*Fourth Book of Maccabees* by Josephus (978-1-63118-562-5)

*The Story of Ahikar* by Ahiqar (978-1-63118-561-8)

**Audio versions are also available on Audible, Amazon and Apple**

# Table of Contents

Introduction...7

*Memory*
By Annie Besant...9

*The Nature of Memory*
By Annie Besant...33

*Memory in the Dying*
By Helena P. Blavatsky...49

# INTRODUCTION

The word "esoteric" can be difficult to define. Esotericism in general can be seen less as a system of beliefs and more as a category, which encompasses numerous, different systems of beliefs. It's a bit of juxtaposition, since the word "esoteric" indicates something that few people know about, while the term itself broadly covers numerous philosophies, practices, areas of study and belief systems.

In a greater sense, Esotericism acts as a storehouse for secret knowledge, which is often considered ancient (by *tradition, if not by fact)*, passed down from generation to generation, in private. At various times in history, simply possessing the knowledge of some of these subjects, was considered illegal and a jailable offence, if discovered. This usually included such general topics as Alchemy, Pharmacology, Qabalah, Hermeticism, Occultism, Ceremonial Magic, Astrology, Divination, Rosicrucianism and so on. Collectively, these areas of study were often referred to as the esoteric sciences.

Sometimes, the outer garment of a subject isn't esoteric, while what is hidden beneath it, is. As an example, Freemasonry isn't necessarily esoteric by nature (at *least not anymore)*, but certain signs, passwords and handshakes given to the candidate during their initiation, are in fact, esoteric, in the sense that they are hidden from the general public.

Today, in the twenty-first century, such topics are readily available at bookstores across the country, and numerous mainsteam publishers offer beginners guides and coffee-table volumes on many of these subjects, intended for mass appeal. Books like *"The Secret"* have turned previously arcane topics into household knowledge. All that being the case, however, it isn't to say that there still aren't buried secrets to uncover, ancient wisdom being ignored and forgotten mysteries to be explored. In fact, it is often that we are only able to further our own studies by standing on the shoulders of these disappearing giants.

Lamp of Trismegistus is doing its part to help preserve humanity's esoteric history by making some of these classics available to those students who are seeking to unearth the knowledge of these ancient colossi.

So, be sure to check other titles from our *Esoteric Classics* series, as well as our *Occult Fiction, Theosophical Classics, Foundations of Freemasonry Series, Supernatural Fiction, Paranormal Research Series, Studies in Buddhism* and our *Christian Apocrypha Series*. You can also download the audio versions of most of these titles from Amazon, Apple or Audible, for learning on the go.

# MEMORY

by Annie Besant

Memory is but a function of the mind, and the answer given to the question, 'What is memory?' must turn on the answer given to the larger question, 'What is mind?' 'Is there a Self or Ego, of which mind, as we know it, is a part; or is mind only the outcome of matter in motion, so that the Self has no real existence? Is mind anything more than an ever changing succession of perceptions and congeries of perceptions, and these the outcome of nervous activity responding to stimuli, peripheral and central? Or is it a definite mode of being, with perceptions *et hoc genus omne* as material on which it works; with faculties whereby it perceives, reproduces, recollects, conceives; but no more as a whole to be identified with its functional activities than the body as a whole consists of eating, breathing or digesting?'

The famous argument of Hume, in the fifth and sixth sections of *A Treatise on Human Nature*, part IV, will be familiar to the student; but I may here recall the results of his introspection:

"For my part, when I enter most intimately into what I call myself, I always stumble on some particular perception or other, of heat or cold, light or shade, pain or pleasure. I never can catch *myself* at any time without a perception. When my perceptions are removed for any time, as by sound sleep, so long am I insensible of *myself*, and may truly be said not to exist. And were all my perceptions removed by death, and I could neither think nor feel, nor see, nor live, nor hate, after the dissolution of my body, I should be entirely annihilated nor can I conceive what is further necessary to make me a perfect non-entity. If anyone, upon superior and unprejudiced reflection, thinks he has a different notion of *himself*, I must confess

I can reason no longer with him. All I can allow him is, that he may be in the right as well as I, and that we are essentially different in this particular. He may, perhaps, perceive something simple and continued which he calls *himself*, though I am certain there is no such principle in me. But, setting aside some metaphysicians of this kind, I may venture to affirm of the rest of mankind, that they are nothing but a bundle or collection of different perceptions, which succeed each other with inconceivable rapidity, and are in a perpetual flux and movement'.

Hume consequently denies the existence of the Self, and explains that the feeling of personal identity arises from the relations between the objects perceived.

## Is Mind a Bundle of Perceptions?

But in reading the whole argument it is impossible to remain unconscious of the self-contradictory nature of the expressions used. 'When I enter ... *I* always stumble upon some perception. 'What is the 'I' that stumbles on a perception, and is able to observe and to recognize it? Is it itself a perception? If so, of what? And can one perception in a 'bundle' perceive other perceptions in the same bundle, and separating itself from its peers scrutinize the remainder and recognize them as a bundle? The argument implies something that observes the perceptions and that assigns to each its rightful name and place. Despite himself, Hume cannot escape from the consciousness that he is other than his perceptions, and this universal result of introspection, the consciousness of the 'I', betrays itself in the very argument aimed at its annihilation. The mind is no more identifiable with its organs than is the brain with the body of which it is a part. It depends on them for its living, and its functioning, but IT IS NOT THEY.

Consider an ordinary perception, say the perception of a chair. Can that perception cognize another, or be anything more than the perception of a chair? If the mind be only a bundle of perceptions, of what nature is the perception that can cognize all the rest, can set itself apart from and above all the rest, and say, ' you are a perception of cold, and you of heat, and you of pain, and you of pleasure'? This perception of perceptions is not very different from the Self that is denied. It is the perceiver, not a perception.

Let anyone experiment on himself; let him shut himself up alone, free from all interruption from without; let him patiently and steadily investigate his mental processes; he will find that the shifting contents of his consciousness are not *he*; that he is other than the feelings, the perceptions, the conceptions that pass before him, that they are his, not he, and that he can drive them away, can empty his mind of all save Self-consciousness, can, in the words of Patanjali, become a 'spectator without a spectacle' .

It may be argued that introspection often yields fallacious results, and that self-observation is the most difficult of all tasks. Granted. So may our senses mislead us, but they are the only guides to the objective world that we possess. Our recognition of their fallibility does not lead us to refuse to use them, but it makes us test their report to the best of our ability, and compare them with the common sense of our race. And so with the result of our inner senses, we test them, compare their reports with those of others; and I venture to say that the common sense [I use the words in the philosophical meaning, the *serisus communis*] of mankind reports the existence of the Self, the permanent Ego amid all the flux of percepts and concepts, and that its existence is as certain as any existence around us in the Object-world.

## Remembering and Forgetting

But we shall judge erroneously of the Self if we only take into account the everyday mental processes, and limit its extent to the extent of the normal waking consciousness. And I know of no study that can throw more light on our true Self than the study of memory, for its phenomena prove to us that Consciousness is something far wider than the consciousness of the moment, as energy, in the physical world, is something more than the forces acting at any given instant of time. Analogy is often useful as throwing light into obscure places, and analogy may serve us here. Physicists speak of energy as 'kinetic' and 'potential', the active and the latent. So consciousness may be active or latent, and the latter division is, for each individual, the greater of the twain. We 'forget', as the phrase goes, more than we 'remember'; but the 'forgotten' has not really passed out of consciousness, though it has become latent, any more than force is absent from the avalanche hanging quiescent on the side of a mountain. The forgotten can be recalled to the active consciousness, and may revolutionize a life as the avalanche may be set free and expend its stored-up energy in laying desolate the valley homes. No force can be annihilated on the physical plane, and no experience destroyed on the mental. That which the normal waking consciousness retains depends on the attention, but a name for a phase of will. That which is best remembered is that which has struck us vividly, *i.e.*, that which has arrested and fixed our attention; or that which has been often repeated so that our attention has been frequently directed to it; in every case the will lies at the root of the retention. Everything that once enters into consciousness leaves thereon its trace; the mind is thereby modified, as Patanjali would phrase it. If this be so the traces should be recoverable, and on this we must challenge the phenomena of memory.

Let us note, at the commencement, that memory has two chief divisions — reproduction and recollection. Reproduction may occur without recollection, and then no recognition will ensue. Memory reproduces the image of a past perception; it will appear to consciousness as new, unless recollection accompanies the reproduction, and instances of this are on record.

'Maury relates that he once wrote an article on political economy for a periodical, but the sheets were mislaid and, therefore, not sent off. He had already forgotten everything that he had written when he was requested to send the promised article. On re-undertaking the work, he thought he had found a completely new point of view for the subject; but when, some months later, the missing sheets were found, it appeared, not only that there was nothing new in his second essay, but that he had repeated his first ideas in almost exactly the same words.' [Maury, *Le Sommeil et les Rêves,* p 440 quoted by du Prel, *Philosophy of Mysticism,* English Translation. vol 2, p 13, trans from German by C C Massey, London 1889] Leibnitz is quoted by du Prel as giving an analogous instance: 'I believe that dreams often renew old thoughts. When Julius Scaliger had celebrated in verse all the famous men of Verona, there appeared to him in a dream one who gave the name of Brugnolus, a Bavarian by birth, who had settled at Verona, complaining that he had been forgotten. Julius Scaliger did not recollect to have heard him spoken of, but upon this dream made elegiac verses in his honour. Afterwards his son, Joseph Scaliger, being on a journey through Italy, learned that formerly there had been at Verona a celebrated grammarian or critic of that name, who had contributed to the restoration of learning in Italy'. [ Ibid pp 14 -15 ] The explanation suggested by Leibnitz is that Scaliger had heard of Brugnolus, but had forgotten him; in the dream, reproduction took place but was not accompanied by recollection, so that the name and character appeared new to Scaliger, and he failed to recognize the dream-presented image. It is impossible to say how much of our dreams may be of this character, and how often the absence of recognition may bestow on them the appearance of revelation. We find ourselves in some place that we have dreamed of, and recognize as real our dream surroundings. Searching our waking consciousness in vain for some record, we rashly conclude that the dream has depicted in some mysterious way an environment unknown to us; whereas it is far more probable that memory has reproduced in our sleeping consciousness the images of perceptions long since forgotten, and recollection failing, they pass before the mind as new.

### Flashbacks before Death

To return to the statement that 'everything that has once entered consciousness leaves thereon its trace'.

In the section on 'Memory of the Dying', some examples are given of the remarkable reproduction, at the end of life, of events and surroundings of childhood, and almost everyone must have come across instances of aged persons who recall with extreme vividness the trivial occurrences of their youth. Dr Winslow [*Diseases of the Brain and Mind,* pages 286-287 ] remarks on some instances in which, 'in very advanced life the faculty of memory exhibits an extraordinary degree of elasticity and a surprising amount of vigour. ... A charming illustration of this fact occurs in the life of Niebuhr, the celebrated Danish traveller. When old, blind, and so infirm that he was able only to be carried from his bed to his chair, he used to describe to his friends the scenes which he had visited in his early days with wonderful minuteness and vivacity. When they expressed their astonishment at the vividness of his memory, he explained 'that as he lay in bed, all visible objects shut out, the pictures of what he had seen in the East continually floated before his mind's eye, so that it was no wonder that he could speak of them as if he had seen them yesterday. With like vividness the deep intense sky of Asia, with its brilliant and twinkling hosts of stars, on which he had so often gazed by night, or its lofty vault of blue by day, was reflected in the hours of stillness and darkness on his inmost soul'.

Yet more remarkable as a proof that that which has passed out of ordinary consciousness is not destroyed, are the many cases on record describing the strange revival of memory, just ere consciousness becomes latent, which is one of the most marked phenomena of drowning. I select the following from Du Prel: [ Op cit vol I, pp 92-93]

At the approach of death, also, the extraordinary exaltation of memory, connected with a change in the measure of time, has been frequently observed. Fechner [*Zentralblatt für Anthropologie und Natur wissenschaft, Jahargang* 1863, p 774] relates the case of a lady who fell into water and was nearly drowned. From the moment when all bodily movement ceased till she was drawn out of the water about two minutes elapsed, during which, according to her own account, she lived again through her whole past, the most insignificant details of it being represented in imagination. Another instance of the same mental action in which the events of whole years were crowded together is described by Admiral Beaufort from his own experience. He had fallen into the water, and had lost (normal) consciousness. In this condition 'thought rose after thought, with a rapidity of succession that is not only indescribable, but probably inconceivable by anyone who has not himself been in a similar situation'. At first, the immediate consequences of his death for his family were presented to him; then, his regards, turned to the past; he repeated his last cruise, an earlier one in which he was shipwrecked, his schooldays, the progress he then made, and the time he had wasted, even all his small childish journeys and adventures. 'Thus travelling backwards, every incident of my past life seemed to me to glance across my recollection in retrograde succession, *not*, however, *in mere outline*, as here stated, but the picture *filled up* with every minute and collateral feature; in short, the whole period of my existence seemed to be placed before me in a kind of *panoramic review*, and every act of it seemed to be accompanied by a consciousness of right and wrong, or by some reflection on its cause or its consequences. Indeed, many trifling events, which had long been forgotten, then crowded into my imagination, and with the character of recent familiarity'. [Haddock, *Somnolism and Psychism,* London 1851 p 213] In this case, also, but two minutes at the most had passed before Beaufort was taken out of the water'.

The approach of death, like extreme old age, will sometimes revive in the memory the impressions of childhood to the obliteration of more recent habits. Dr Winslow [ Loc.cit., P.320] quotes Dr Rush as recording a statement of the Rev. Dr Muhlenberg, of Lancaster, USA, who 'alluding to the German emigrants over whom he exercised pastoral care, observes, 'people generally pray shortly before death in their native language. This is a fact that I have found true in innumerable cases among my German hearers, although hardly one word of their native language was spoken by them in common life and when in health'.

### Memory Stimulated by Disease

Passing attacks of disease will alter the contents of memory in the most remarkable way, so that the view seems wellnigh forced upon us that the consciousness retains *all* impressions, but that the threshold below which all is latent, shifts, as it were, up and down, now letting some images appear in the active consciousness and now others. The following three illustrative cases are from Dr Winslow's work. [Op. cit. pp 320-321] 'Dr Hutchinson refers to the case of a physician who had in early life renounced the principles of the Roman Catholic Church. During an attack of delirium which preceded his death he prayed only in the forms of the Church of

Rome, while all recollection of the prescribed formulae of the Protestant religion was effaced and obliterated from the mind by the cerebral infection. A gentleman was thrown from his horse while hunting. He was taken from the field to a neighbouring cottage in a state of unconsciousness, and was subsequently removed to his own residence. For the period of a week his life was considered in imminent danger. When he was sufficiently restored to enable him to articulate, he began to talk German, a language he had acquired in early life, but had not spoken for nearly twenty-five years . . . A gentleman had a serious attack of illness. When restored, it was found that he had lost all recollection of recent circumstances, but had a lucid memory as to events that had occurred in *early life*, in fact, impressions, that had long been forgotten, were again revived. As this patient recovered his bodily health, a singular alteration was observed in the character of his memory. He again recollected *recent* ideas, but entirely forgot all the events of past years'..

Another class of proofs of the permanence of impressions on the consciousness may be drawn from the recorded cases of the exaltation of memory, which frequently accompanies disease and abnormal conditions of the nervous system. Du Prel has collected a large number of instances, from which I take the following: [ Loc. cit vol 2, pp 19, 21-28 ]

'Coleridge mentions a maid-servant who, in the delirium of fever, recited long passages in Hebrew which she did not understand, and could not repeat when in health, but which formerly, when in the service of a priest, she had heard him deliver aloud. She also quoted passages from theological works, in Latin and Greek, which she only half understood, when the priest, as was his custom, read aloud his favourite authors on going to and from church. [ Maudsley, *Physiology and Pathology of the Soul,* p.14 ]. A Rostock peasant, in a fever, suddenly recited the Greek words commencing the Gospel of St John, which he had accidentally heard sixty years before; and Benecke mentions a peasant woman who, in fever, uttered Syriac, Chaldean and Hebrew words which, when a little girl, she had accidentally heard in the house of a scholar . . . [Radestock, *Schlaj und Traum*, p.136] A deranged person, who was cured by Dr Willis, said that in his attacks his memory attained extraordinary power, so that long passages from Latin authors occurred to him . . . [Reil, Raphsodien p.304] A girl of seven, employed as neatherd [Cowherd], occupied a room divided only by a thin partition from that of a violin player, who often gave himself up to his favourite pursuit during half the night. Some months later, the girl got another place, in which she had already been for two years, when frequently in the night tones exactly like those, of the violin were heard coming from her room, but which were produced by the sleeping girl herself. This often went on for hours, sometimes with interruptions, after which she would continue the song where she had left off. With irregular intervals, this lasted for two years. Then she reproduced also the tones of a piano which was played in the family, and afterwards she began to speak, and held forth with remarkable acuteness on political and religious subjects, often in a very accomplished and sarcastic way; she also conjugated Latin, or spoke like a tutor to a pupil. In all which cases this entirely ignorant girl merely reproduced what had been said by members of the family or visitors'.

I have quoted this last case in order to draw attention to the significant fact that sleep may cause the shifting of the threshold, as well as sickness or insanity.

Dr Winslow [ loc. cit. pp.336-338 ] gives some cases of extraordinary memory, characterizing incipient brain-disease, and he also records many curious instances of double consciousness, in which the patient practically lives a double life, remembering in each state only those incidents which occurred in it. [ Pp.332-338] Here, again, we seem to be confronted with the shifting threshold as the only tenable hypothesis.

Persons under hypnotism frequently exhibit an extreme exaltation of memory, repeating long passages read to them but once, recalling with accuracy long past and trivial events, describing minutely the insignificant occurrences of many successive days. Many instances of this kind will be found by the student in Binet and Féré's *Animal Magnetism*, and in Dr Richer's *Études sur la grande Hystérie*.

With this rough survey of the field of memory in our minds, we must seek for some hypothesis which will resume the facts, and which, tested by fresh experiments, will explain other memory-phenomena. I put Humes hypothesis out of court, and proceed to consider the materialistic and theosophical theories of memory, to answer the question whether memory is a function of matter in motion, or a faculty of the Self functioning *through* matter, but not resultant from it.

### The Materialistic Theory of Memory

According to this theory, memory, like all other mental functions, is the result of the vibrations of the brain nerve-cells, and may be expressed in terms of matter and motion. When a stimulus from the object-world sets up a vibration in a sense-organ, that vibration is propagated as a wave from cell to cell of the nervous chain till it reaches its appropriate center in the cerebrum. There arises the perception, the outcome of *mental* activity. This nervous action, once set up, tends to repeat itself more easily with each similar stimulus, the nervous energy following the path of least resistance and each occurrence of the similar vibration making easier further repetition. Such a vibration having once been set up, it may recur in the absence of the external stimulus, and we have the idea in lieu of the sensation-perception. Whenever the nerve cells vibrate as they vibrated under the first stimulus, the ideas recur, and this recurrence is termed memory. Now, when the vibration is first set up, it is at its strongest, and it is argued that this intensity of vibration lessens until it is not sufficient to affect the consciousness. Mr James Ward writes: [*Journal and Speculative Philosophy,* vol xvii no 2 quoted by Sully, *Outlines of Psychology.*]

'What now do we know of this central image in the intervals when it is not consciously presented? Manifestly our knowledge in this case can only be inferential at the best. But there are two facts, the importance of which Herbart was the first to see, from which we may learn something. I refer to what he calls the rising and falling of presentations. All presentations having more than a limited intensity rise gradually to a maximum and gradually decline: and when they have fallen below the threshold of consciousness altogether, the process seems to continue; for the longer the time that elapses before their 'revival', the fainter they appear when revived, and the more slowly they rise. This evanescence is more rapid at first, becoming less as the intensity of the presentation diminishes. It is too much to say that this holds with mathematical accuracy, although Herbart has gone this length. Still, it is true enough to suggest the notion that an object, even when it is no longer able to influence attention, continues to be presented, though with ever less and less absolute intensity, till at length its intensity declines to an almost dead level just above zero. Put into the materialistic language this would be that the nervous elements vibrate at first strongly and continue to vibrate, with less and less vigour, until the vibration is insufficient to affect the consciousness, and the image sinks below the threshold. The vibrations go on, still diminishing, but *not* ceasing; if they cease the image is lost beyond revival; if they continue, however feebly, they may be reinforced and once more rise to an intensity which lifts them above the threshold of consciousness. Such reinforcement is due to association. As Sully put it very clearly: [*Outlines of Psychology*, pp 236-237 ]

'In order to understand more precisely what is meant by the Law of Contiguous Association, we may let A and B stand for two impressions [percepts] occurring together, and *a* and *b* for the two representations answering to these. Then the Law asserts that when A [or *a*] recurs it will tend to excite or call up *b*; and similarly that the recurrence of B [or *b*] will tend to excite *a*. . . The physiological explanation of this association seems to be the fact that two nerve structures that have repeatedly acted together acquire a disposition to act in combination in the same way. This fact is explained by the hypothesis that such a conjoint action of two nerve centers somehow tends to fix the line of nervous excitation or nervous discharge when one center is again stimulated in the direction of the other. In other words, paths of connection are formed between the two regions. But it may be doubted whether physiologists can as yet give a satisfactory account of the nervous concomitants of the associative process.

## The Physiological Side

Lewes defines memory on the physiological side as 'an organized tendency to react on lines previously traversed' [*The Physical Basis of Mind* ]; and Herbert Spencer relates each class of feelings to its own group of cells [vesicles] in the brain. He says:

'f the association of each feeling with its general class answers to the localisation of the corresponding nervous action within the great nervous mass in which all feelings of that class arise' if the association of this feeling with its sub-class answers to the localisation of the nervous action within that part of this great nervous mass in which feelings of this sub-class arise, and so on to the end with the smallest groups of feelings and smallest clusters of nerve-vesicles; then, to what answers the association of each feeling with predecessors identical in kind? It answers to the re-excitation of the particular vesicle or vesicles which, when before excited, yielded the like feeling before experienced; the appropriate stimulus having set up in certain vesicles the molecular changes which they undergo when disturbed, there is aroused a feeling of the same quality with feelings previously aroused when such stimuli set up such changes in these vesicles. And the association of feeling with the preceding like feelings corresponds to the physical re-excitation of the same structures'. [*The Principles of Psychology*. London 1831 vol I, p 258]

We are then to regard memory as the result of the re-excitation of vesicles of the brain the theory is clear and definite enough. Is it true?

The first difficulty that arises is the limited space available for the containment of these vesicles, and the consequent limitation of their number. It is true that their possible combinations may be practically infinite in number, but this does not help us; for they are to continually vibrate, however feebly, so long as an idea is capable of revival, and a vesicle vibrating simultaneously in some thousands of combinations would be in a parlous molecular condition. For all these combinations must exist simultaneously, and each must maintain its inter-related vibrations without cessation. Now, is this possible? It is true that from the vibrating strings of a piano you may get myriads of combinations of notes; but you cannot have all these combinations sounding from the strings at the same time, some loud and some soft, some forcible and some feeble. By keeping the loud pedal down you may keep some combinations going for a short time, while you produce fresh vibrations; but what is the effect? A blurred confusion of sounds, causing an intolerable discord. If we are to explain memory under the laws of matter in motion, we must accept the consequences deducible from these laws, and these consequences are inconsistent with the facts of memory as we know them. Any attempt to represent clearly in consciousness the physical concomitants of memory as merely the outcome of vibrating nervous elements will prove to the student the impossibility of the hypothesis. The brain is a sufficiently wonderful mechanism as the organ of mind; as the creator of mind it is inconceivable.

Du Prel [*Philosophy of Mysticism*, vol 2, pp 108-109] helps us to realize the difficulties enveloping the materialistic hypothesis. On this hypothesis 'Memory' would depend on material brain-traces, left behind by impressions; by the act of memory such traces are continually renewed, rechiselled as it were, and so there arise well-worn tracks [Herbert Spencer's 'lines of least resistance'], 'in which the coach of memory is conducted with especial facility'. And he adds:

'The deductions from this view had already been drawn by the materialists of the last century. Hook and others recognized that, since one-third of a second sufficed for the production of an impression, in one hundred years a man must have collected in his brain 9,467,180,000 traces or copies of impressions, or, reduced by one-third for the period of sleep, 3,155,760,000; thus in fifty years, 1,577,880,000; further that, allowing a weight of four pounds to the brain, and subtracting one pound for blood and vessels and another for the external integument, a single grain of brain substance must contain 205,542 traces.. . . Moreover, our intellectual life does not consist in mere impressions; these form only the material of our judgment. These brain-atoms do not help us to judgment, notwithstanding their magical properties, so that we must suppose that whenever we form a sentence or a judgment the impressions are combined, like the letters in a compositor's box, these atoms however, being at the same time compositor and box'.

There is another result that would follow from memory being only the outcome of vibrating cells, and I may be permitted to quote it from my essay on hypnotism: 'Memory is the faculty which receives the impressions of our experiences and preserves them; many of these impressions fade away, and we say we have forgotten. Yet it is clear that these impressions may be revived. They are, therefore, not destroyed, but are so faint that they sink below the threshold of consciousness, and so no longer form part of its normal content. If thought be but a 'mode of motion', memory must be similarly regarded; but it is not possible to conceive that each impression of our past life, recorded in consciousness, is still vibrating in the same group of cells, only so feebly that it does not rise over the threshold. For these same cells are continually being thrown into groupings for new vibrations, and these cannot all co-exist, and the fainter ones be each capable of receiving fresh impulse which may so intensify their motion as to raise them again into consciousness. Now if these vibrations = Memory, if we have only matter in motion, we know the laws of dynamics sufficiently well to say that if a body be set vibrating, and new forces be successively brought to act on it and set up new vibrations, there will not be in that body the co-existence of each separate set of vibrations successively impressed upon it, but it will vibrate in a way differing from each single set and compounded of all. So that memory as a mode of motion, would not give us the record of the past, but would present us with a new story, the resultant of all those past vibrations, and this would be ever changing as new impressions, causing new vibrations, come in to modify the resultant of the whole'. If the reader have in mind the phenomena of memory given in the earlier part of this essay; if he note that these seem to imply that we forget *nothing*, *i.e.*, that every vibration caused throughout the life persists;

if, remembering this, he once more attempts to represent clearly in consciousness the brain-condition required by this theory, is it too much to say that he will be compelled to admit that it is inconceivable?

Nor can we forget that there is a certain race-memory, wrought into our physical organisms, which still further complicates the work to be accomplished by these over-burdened vesicles. This unconscious memory of the body, derived from physical inheritance, cannot be wholly thrown out of account when we deal with cell-vibrations.

## The Theosophical Theory of Memory

Here I must guard myself. I cannot really put forward the theosophical theory, for I do not find it set out in any work that I have read. I can only suggest a theory, which seems to me, as a student of Theosophy, to be fairly deducible from the constitution of man as laid down in theosophical treatises. We learn to distinguish between the true individuality, the Ego, and the temporary personality that clothes it. The Ego is the conscious, the thinking agent. It is the Ego of whom the mind forms part, one of whose functions is memory. Every event that occurs passes into the consciousness of the Ego and is there stored up; the past is thus for it ever the present, since all is present in consciousness. [All is present in eternal ideation *Alaya*, the universal soul and consciousness - we are taught; and the higher Ego [*Manas*] is the first-born of *Alaya* or *Mahat*, being called *Manasaputra* = 'Son of Mind'.] But how far the Ego can impress its knowledge on the brain of the physical organism with which it is connected, and thus cause this knowledge to enter the consciousness of the person concerned, must, in the nature of the case, depend on the condition of the organism at the moment, and the laws within which it works. What we call the threshold of consciousness divides what is 'remembered' from what is 'forgotten'. All above the threshold is within the personal consciousness, while all below this threshold is outside it. But this threshold belongs to the personal consciousness, and 'here is the significant point' varies with the material conditions of the moment. It is movable, not fixed and the contents of consciousness vary with the movement of the threshold. Thus:

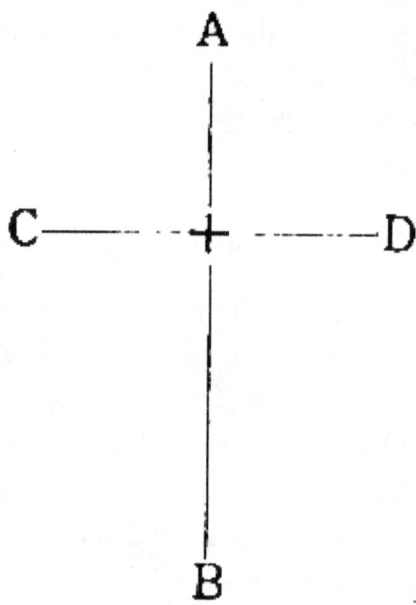

Let A B represent the consciousness of the Ego; let C D represent the threshold of consciousness of the person; of all above C D the person will be conscious, it will be impressed on the material brain; of all below C D he will be unconscious. But if C D be movable upwards and downwards, the contents of his consciousness will vary with its movement, and he will remember or forget according as the idea is above or below this dividing line. [We have to exclude from this the impressions of a purely physical nature, such as enter in the category of *animal* perception and memory. Such impressions reach the human Ego, and it cannot fail to note them; but they do not impress themselves indelibly on *its*

consciousness, and can never, therefore, follow the Ego to Devachan.]

## Waking and Dreaming Consciousness

Now the condition of the organism is constantly varying; but there are two states of consciousness that occur in everyone and are, clearly distinguishable 'the waking consciousness and the dream consciousness. The contents of these differ to a remarkable extent, and they work under curiously different conditions. The waking consciousness works under conditions of time and space; the dream consciousness is free from them — it can live through years in a second of time, it can annihilate space in its movements. In the dream the place of the dreamer depends on his thought, he is where he thinks himself. Not only so, but the dream consciousness often retains events erased from the waking memory. Let the reader turn back to pages 8 and 9, and note the curious phenomena of reproduction without recollection in the dream state. Is it an impossible theory that when the senses are closed to the object-world, when the bodily functions have touched their lowest activity, then the Ego may be able to impress on this negative organism far more of its own contents than it can impress upon it when in its more vigorous state? Does it not seem as though that which is below the threshold of the waking consciousness becomes that which is above the threshold of the dream consciousness, and as though the double life of waking and sleeping is but the activity of the one Ego working under the contrasted physical conditions?

If this be not so, we seem to be driven to the conception of a duality at the very centre of being; each man is not one, but twain, in the innermost recesses of consciousness.

On the other hand, the theory for which I contend leaves the individuality single, varying in its manifestations according to the physical conditions through which it works; and all the strange cases of double consciousness, which have so perplexed the physiologist and the psychologist, together with the phenomena of somnambulism, mesmerism, hypnotism, and similar conditions, fall into line as severally belonging to one of the two states of consciousness, the dream and the waking, the Ego working equally in either, but conditioned in turn by each.

'Ordinary sleep' as du Prel says, 'is a condition intermediate between waking and somnambulism, the latter being only its exaltation'. In this connection these facts are to be noted; if we sleep lightly and dream, we remember our dreams; if we sleep more soundly, we sometimes remember the dream more vividly on waking, but in an hour or two we have completely forgotten it and cannot revive the memory, try as we may; in deep sleep we dream, as has often been discovered by closely watching a person wrapped in profound slumber, but no trace remains on our waking memory. In somnambulism, which is closely allied to this deep sleep, no memory persists, as a rule, into a waking state. A person who is a somnambulist lives a double life; sleeping, he remembers his sleep experiences and sometimes his waking ones; waking he remembers only his waking life. Occasionally, but only rarely, the golden bridge of memory spans the gulf between the waking and the somnambulic consciousness, dreams sometimes interposing as connecting link between the two. It must be remembered that a somnambulist, left to himself, will pass into ordinary sleep before awaking, and when this is the case dream may carry on memory of the somnambulist into the waking state.

## Transcendental Consciousness

Du Prel puts very clearly the existence of what he calls the 'transcendental consciousness', which has much in common, though it is not identical with, the theosophical Ego:

'There can be no right theory of remembering without the right theory of forgetting. The phenomenon of alternating consciousness shows that very clearly. It is only when we know what becomes of an impression which is forgotten, that we can answer the question whence it comes to memory. Now, what is the process of forgetting? It is a disappearance from the normal sense consciousness. There can be no destruction of the impression, or its reproduction would be impossible. Excluding the brain-trace theory, there must be a psychical organ, preserving *the faculty of reproduction*, even if the impression, as product of its *earlier* activity, should be destroyed. This organ, lying beyond the self- consciousness, belongs to the unconscious. If, however, this organ had simply the latent faculty of reproduction, and did not rather draw into itself and preserve unchanged the impression as product, we should have again within this organ to distinguish between the conscious and the unconscious. The hypothesis would thus explain nothing, the difficulty being merely pushed back and transposed. There is therefore, no alternative but to say that this organ is not in itself at all unconscious, but only so from the standpoint of the sense-consciousness; that it is not merely a latent faculty of reproduction but takes up into *its* consciousness the impression, as the latter disappears from the external consciousness. By this admission of a transcendental consciousness, the possibility of memory is explained by the mere transposition of the psycho-physical threshold with every retreat of the boundary between the sense and the transcendental consciousness. If a forgotten impression sank into a real unconscious, it would not be apparent how in memory this unconscious should suddenly become again conscious. The forgotten, therefore, cannot thereby cease to belong to a consciousness, and since forgetting is the disappearance from the sense-consciousness, we must admit the existence of a second. And so, to say that an impression is forgotten means that it has passed over from the sense-consciousness to the transcendental. [Op cit vol 2, pp 111 -13].

## Hyper-Ethereal

The answer to this that would leap to the lips of the materialist is that the impression 'goes' nowhere, any more than motion 'goes' anywhere when a wheel is stopped. But this obvious answer leaves out important facts in the case. The motion is changed into another form of physical energy, as heat caused by the friction which stops it, and the wheel cannot reproduce the motion; the new impulse to move must come from a living force without it. Now the impression *is* revivable, without any external action, by Self- action, and the materialist theory of memory implies its continual production by ceaselessly vibrating vesicles, albeit the vibrations be not vigorous enough to attract attention.

If we admit the existence of the Ego, personal memory would be the power of the personal brain to receive impressions from it; to respond, so to speak, to the subtler vibrations of, perhaps, the 'thought- stuff' of which Clifford dreamed. Comparing the vibrations of our gross forms of matter with the vibrations of the ether we can reason by analogy to a form of matter as much subtler than nerve-matter of our brain. There, indeed, may be the possibility of vibrations such as are necessary to make our thought process conceivable. At present, this can only be a hypothesis to us, but it is a hypothesis which throws light on this obscure subject, and may be provisionally accepted, until further researches prove or disprove it.

Here will find their justification all attempts to refine and increase the sensitiveness of the nerve-matter of the brain, for increased delicacy will mean increased faculty of responding to the hyper-ethereal vibrations that is, it will enable the Ego to impress on our personal consciousness more and more the contents of his own.

By this theory we can understand the exalted mental faculties of the somnambulist, the tension of the nervous system rendering it more sensitive, *i.e.*, more responsive. By it we can understand the danger of the ignorant striving after this abnormal condition, the nervous elements becoming exhausted by over-rapid discharge and excessive strain. 'Great wits to madness often are allied' is only too true; the sensitiveness which is genius may easily pass into the hyper-sensitiveness that is insanity.

And so we reach the practical conclusion — to walk warily in these little-trodden realms, because there is a danger; but to walk, because without courage to face the darkness no light can come.

# THE NATURE OF MEMORY

by Annie Besant

The nature of memory is a problem which has been troubling theosophical students for many years, and perhaps I may also succeed in troubling them still further by offering a theory on the subject; on the other hand it is possible that I may succeed in helping them a little by the presentation of a view that is to myself helpful and clarifying.

What is memory? How does it work? By what means do we recover the past, whether near or remote? For, after all, whether the past be near or remote, belonging to this or to any anterior life, the means which govern its recovery must be similar, and we require a theory which will include all cases of memory, and at the same time will enable us to understand each particular case.

The first step towards obtaining a definite and intelligible theory is a comprehension of our own composition, of the Self with its sheaths, and their inter-relation. We must bear constantly in mind the facts that our consciousness is a unit, and that this unit of consciousness works through various sheaths, which impose upon it a false appearance of multiplicity. The innermost, or most tenuous, of these sheaths is inseparable from the unit of consciousness; in fact, it is this sheath which makes it a unit. This unit is the Monad, dwelling on the Anupadaka plane; but for all practical purposes we may take it as the familiar inner Man, the Tri-Atom, Atma-Buddhi-Manas, thought of as apart from the Atmic, Buddhic and Manasic sheaths. This unit of consciousness manifests through, abides in, sheaths belonging to the five planes of its activity, and we call it the Self working in its sheaths.

We must think, then, of a conscious Self dwelling in vehicles that vibrate. The vibrations of these vehicles correspond, on the side of matter, with the changes in consciousness in the side of the Self. We cannot accurately speak of vibrations of consciousness, because vibrations can only belong to the material side of things, the form side, and only loosely can we speak of a vibrating consciousness corresponding with vibrations in sheaths.

The question of the vehicles, or bodies, in which consciousness, the Self, is working, is all-important as regards memory. The whole process of recovering more or less remote events is a question of picturing them in the sheath 'of shaping part of the matter of the sheath into their likeness' in which consciousness is working at the time. In the Self, as a fragment of the universal Self ' which for our purpose we can take to be the LOGOS, although in verity the LOGOS is but a portion of the universal Self' is present in everything; for in the universal Self is present all which has taken place, is taking place, and will take place in the universe; all this, and an illimitable more is present in the universal Consciousness. Let us think only of a universe and its LOGOS. We speak of Him as omnipresent and omniscient. Now, fundamentally, that omnipresence and omniscience are in the individualized Self, as being one with the LOGOS, but 'we must put in here a but' with a difference; the difference consisting in this, that while in the separated Self, as Self, apart from all vehicles, that omnipresence and omniscience reside by virtue of his unity with the one Self, the vehicles in which he dwells have not yet learned to vibrate in answer to his change of consciousness, as he turns his attention to one or another part of his contents. Hence we say that all exists in him potentially, and not as in the LOGOS actually: all the changes which go on in the consciousness of the LOGOS are reproducible in this separated Self, which is an indivisible part of His life, but the vehicles are not yet ready as media of manifestation. Because of the separation of form, because of this closing in of the separate, or individualized, Self, these possibilities which are within it as part of the Universal Self are latent, not manifest, are possibilities, not actualities. As in every atom which goes to the making up of a vehicle, there are illimitable possibilities of vibration, so in every separated Self there are illimitable possibilities of changes of consciousness.

## Self is One with Logos

We do not find in the atom, at the beginning of a solar system, an illimitable variety of vibrations; but we learn that it possesses a capacity to acquire an illimitable variety of vibrations; it acquires these in the course of its evolution, as it responds continually to vibrations playing upon its surface; at the end of a solar system, an immense number of the atoms in it have reached the stage of evolution in which they can vibrate in answer to any vibration touching them that arises within the system; then, for that system, these atoms are said to be perfected. The same thing is true for the separated, or individualized, Selves. All the changes taking place in the consciousness of the LOGOS which are represented in that universe, and take shape as forms in that universe, all these are also within the perfected consciousness in that universe, and any of these changes can be reproduced in any one of them. Here is memory: the re- appearance, the re-incarnation in matter, of anything that has been within that universe, and therefore ever is, in the consciousness of its LOGOS, and in the consciousness which are part of His consciousness. Although we think of the Self as separate as regards all other Selves, we must ever remember it is in-separate as regards the ONE SELF, the LOGOS. His life is not shut out from any part of His universe, and in Him we live and move and have our being, open ever to Him, filled with His life.

As the Self puts on vehicle after vehicle of matter, its powers of gaining knowledge become, with each additional vehicle, more circumscribed but also more definite. Arrived on the physical plane, consciousness is narrowed down to the experiences which can be received through the physical body, and chiefly through those openings which we call the sense-organs; these are avenues through which knowledge can reach the imprisoned Self, though we often speak of them as shutting out knowledge when we think of the capacities of the subtler vehicles. The physical body renders perception definitive and clear much as a screen with a minute hole in it allows a picture of the outside world to appear on a screen that would otherwise show a blank surface; rays of light are truly shut off from the screen, but by that very shutting off, those allowed to enter form a clearly defined picture.

Let us now see what happens as regards the physical vehicle in the reception of an impression and in the subsequent recall of that impression, *i.e.*, in the memory of it.

A vibration from outside strikes on an organ of sense, and is transmitted to the appropriate centre in the brain. A group of cells in the brain vibrates, and that vibration leaves the cells in a state somewhat different from the one in which they were previous to its reception. The trace of that response is a possibility for the group of cells; it has once vibrated in a particular way, and it retains for the rest of its existence as a group of cells the possibility of again vibrating in that same way without again receiving a stimulus from the outside world. Each repetition of an identical vibration strengthens this possibility, each leaving its own trace, but many such repetitions will be required to establish a self-initiated repetition: the cells come nearer to this possibility of a self-initiated vibration by each repetition compelled from outside. But this vibration has not stopped with the physical cells; it has been transmitted inwards to the corresponding cell, or group of cells, in the subtler vehicles, and has ultimately produced a change in consciousness. This change, in its turn, re-acts on the cells, and a repetition of the vibrations is initiated from within by the change in consciousness, and this repetition is a memory of the object which started the series of vibrations. The response of the cells to the vibration from outside, a response compelled by the laws of the physical universe, gives to the cells the power of responding to a similar impulse, though feebler, coming from within. A little power is exhausted in each moving of matter in a new vehicle, and hence a gradual diminution of the energy in the vibration. Less and less is exhausted as the cells repeat similar vibrations in response to new impacts from without, the cells answering more readily with each repetition.

Therein lies the value of the 'without'. It wakes up in the matter, more easily than by any other way, the possibility of response, being more closely akin to the vehicles than the 'within'.

The change caused in consciousness, also, leaves the consciousness more ready to repeat that change than it was at first to yield to it, and each such change brings the consciousness nearer to the power to initiate a similar change. Looking back into the dawnings of consciousness, we see that the imprisoned Selves go through innumerable experiences before a Self-initiated change in consciousness occurs; but bearing this in mind, as a fact, we can leave these early stages, and study the workings of consciousness at a more advanced point. We must also remember that every impact, reaching the innermost sheath and giving rise to a change in consciousness, is followed by a reaction, the change in consciousness causing a new series of vibrations from within outwards; there is the going inwards to the Self, followed by the rippling outwards from the Self, the first due to the object, and giving rise to what we call a perception, and the second due to the reaction of the Self, causing what we call a memory.

## Memories of Past Lives

A number of sense-impressions, coming through sight, hearing, touch, taste and smell, run up from the physical vehicle through the astral to the mental. There they are co-ordinated into a complex unity, as a musical chord is composed of many notes. This is the special work of the mental body: it receives many streams and synthesizes them into one; it builds many impressions into a perception, a thought, a complex unity.

Let us try to catch this complex thing after it has gone inwards and has caused a change in consciousness, an idea; the change it has caused gives rise to new vibrations in the vehicles, reproducing those it had caused on its inward way, and in each vehicle it reappears in a fainter form. It is not strong, vigorous and vivid, as when its component parts flashed from the physical to the astral, and from the astral to the mental; it reappears in the mental in a fainter form, the copy of that which the mental sent inward, but the vibrations feebler; as the Self receives from it a reaction — for the impact of a vibration on touching each vehicle *must* cause a re-action — that re-action is far feebler than the original action, and will therefore seem less 'real' than that action; it makes a lesser change in consciousness, and that lessening represents inevitably a less 'reality'

So long as the consciousness is too little responsive to be aware of any impacts that do not come through with the impulsive vigour of the physical, it is literally more in touch with the physical than with any other sheath, and there will be no memories of ideas, but only memories of perceptions, *i.e.*, of pictures of outside objects, caused by vibrations of the nervous matter of the brain, reproducing themselves in the related astral and mental matter. These are literally pictures in the mental matter, as are the pictures on the retina of the eye. And the consciousness perceives these pictures, 'sees' them, as we may truly say, since the seeing of the eye is only a limited expression of its perceptive power. As the consciousness draws a little away from the physical, turning attention more to the modification in its inner sheaths, it sees these pictures reproduced in the brain from the astral sheath by its own re-action passing outwards, and there is the memory of sensations. The picture arises in the brain by the re-action of the change in consciousness, and is recognized there. This recognition implies that the consciousness has withdrawn largely from the physical to the astral vehicle, and is working therein. The human consciousness is thus working at the present time, and is, therefore full of memories, these memories being reproductions in the physical brain of past pictures, caused by re-actions from consciousness. In a lowly evolved human type, these pictures are pictures of past events in which the physical body was concerned, memories of hunger and thirst and of their gratification, of sexual pleasures, and so on, things in which the physical body took an active part. In a higher type, in which the consciousness is working more in the mental vehicle, the pictures in the astral body will draw more of its attention; these pictures are shaped in the astral body by the vibrations coming outwards from the mental, and are perceived as pictures by the consciousness as it withdraws itself more into the mental body as its immediate vehicle. As this process goes on, and the more awakened consciousness responds to vibrations initiated from outside on the astral plane by astral objects, these objects grow 'real' and become distinguishable from the memories, the pictures in the astral body caused by the re-actions from consciousness.

Let us note, in passing, that with the memory of an object goes hand in hand a picture of the renewal of the keener experience of the object by physical contact, and this we call anticipation; and the more complete the memory of an event the more complete is this anticipation. So that the memory will sometimes even cause in the physical body the re-actions which normally accompany the contact with the external object, and we may savor in anticipation pleasures which are not within present reach of the body. Thus the anticipation of savory food will cause 'the mouth to water.' This fact will again appear, when we reach the completion of our theory of memory.

Now, having noted the changes in the vehicles which arise from impacts from the external world, the response to these as changes of consciousness, the feebler vibrations produced in the vehicles by the re-action of consciousness, and the recognition of these again by consciousness as memories, let us come to the crux of the question: What is memory? The breaking up of the bodies between death and reincarnation puts an end to their automatism, to their power of responding to vibrations similar to those already experienced; the responsive groups are disintegrated, and all that remains as a seed for future responses is stored within the permanent atoms; how feeble this is, as compared with the new automatisms imposed on the mass of the bodies by new experiences of the external, may be judged by the absence of any memory of past lives initiated in the vehicles themselves. In fact, all the permanent atoms can do is to answer more readily to vibrations of a kind similar to those previously experienced than to those that come to them for the first time. The memory of the cells, or of groups of cells, perishes at death, and cannot be said to be recoverable, as such. Where then is memory preserved?

The brief answer is: memory is not a faculty and is not preserved; it does not inhere in consciousness as a capacity, nor is any memory of events stored up in the individual consciousness. Every event is a present fact in the universe-consciousness, in the consciousness of the LOGOS; everything that occurs in His universe, past, present and future, is ever there in His all-embracing consciousness, in His 'eternal Now'. From the beginning of the universe to its ending, from its dawn to its sunset, all is there, ever-present, existent. In that ocean of ideas, all IS; we, wandering in the ocean, touch fragments of its contents, and our response to the contact is our knowledge; having known, we can more readily again contact, and this repetition ' when falling short of the contact of the outside sheath of the moment with the fragments occupying its own plane' is memory. All 'memories' are recoverable because all possibilities of image-producing vibrations are within the consciousness of the LOGOS, and we can share in that consciousness the more easily as we have previously shared more often similar vibrations; hence, the vibrations which have formed parts of our experience are more readily repeated by us than those we have never known, and here comes in the value of the permanent atoms; the thrill out again, on being stimulated, the vibrations previously performed, and out of all the possibilities of vibrations of the atoms and molecules of our bodies those sound out which answer to the note struck by the permanent atoms. The fact that we have been affected vibrationally and by changes of consciousness during the present life makes it easier for us to take out of the universal consciousness that of which we have already had experience in our own. Whether it be a memory in the present life, or one in a life long past, the method of recovery is the same. There is no memory save the ever-present consciousness of the LOGOS, in whom we literally live and move and have our being; and our memory is merely putting ourselves into touch with such parts of His consciousness as we have previously shared.

Hence, according to Pythagoras, all learning is remembrance, for it is the drawing from the consciousness of the LOGOS into that of the separated Self that which in our essential unity with Him is eternally ours. On the plane where the unity overpowers the separateness, we share His consciousness of our universe; on the lower planes, where the separateness veils the unity, we are shut out therefrom by our unevolved vehicles. It is the lack of responsiveness in these which hinders us, for we can only know the planes through them. Therefore we cannot directly improve our memory; we can only improve our general receptivity and power to reproduce, by rendering our bodies more sensitive, while being careful not to go beyond their limit of elasticity. Also we can 'pay attention'; *i.e.*, we can turn the awareness of consciousness, we can concentrate consciousness on that special part of the consciousness of the LOGOS to which we desire to attune ourselves. We need not thus distress ourselves with calculations as to 'how many angels can stand on the point of a needle', how we can preserve in a limited space the illimitable number of vibrations experienced in many lives; for the whole of the form-producing vibrations in the universe are ever-present, and are available to be drawn upon by any individual unit, and can be reached as, by evolution, such a one experiences ever more and more.

Let us apply this to an event in our past life. Some of the circumstances 'remain in our memory', others are 'forgotten'. Really, the event exists with all its surrounding circumstances, 'remembered' and 'forgotten' alike, in but one state, the memory of the LOGOS, the universal memory. Anyone who is able to place himself in touch with that memory can recover the whole circumstances as much as we can; *the events through which we have passed* are not ours but form part of the contents of His consciousness; and our sense of property in them is only due to the fact that we have previously vibrated to them, and therefore vibrate again to them more readily than if we contacted them for the first time.

We may, however, contact them with different sheaths at different times, living as we do under time and space conditions which vary with each sheath. The part of the consciousness of the LOGOS that we move through in our physical bodies is far more restricted than that we move through in our astral and mental bodies, and the contacts through a well-organized body are far more vivid than those through a less-organized one. Moreover, it must be remembered that the restriction of area is due to our vehicles only; faced by the complete event, physical, astral, mental, spiritual, our consciousness of it is limited within the range of the vehicles able to respond to it. We feel ourselves *to be* among the circumstances which surround the grossest vehicle we are acting in, and which thus touch it from 'outside'; whereas we 'remember' the circumstances which we contact with the fine vehicles, these transmitting the vibrations to the grosser vehicle, which is thus touched from 'within'.

## Test of Objectivity

The test of objectivity that we apply to circumstances 'present' or 'remembered' is that of the 'common sense'. If others around us see as we see, hear as we hear, we regard the circumstances as objective; if they do not, if they are unconscious of that of which we are conscious, we regard the circumstances as subjective. But this test of objectivity is only valid for those who are active in the same sheaths; if one person is working in the physical body and another in the physical and the astral, the things objective to the man in the astral body cannot affect the man in the physical body, and he will declare them to be subjective hallucinations. The 'common sense' can only work in similar bodies; it will give similar results when all are in physical bodies, all in astral, or all in mental. For the 'common sense' is merely the thought-forms of the LOGOS on each plane, conditioning each embodied consciousness, and enabling it to respond by certain changes to certain vibrations in its vehicles. It is by no means confined to the physical plane, but the average humanity at the present stage of evolution has not sufficiently unfolded the indwelling consciousness for them to exercise any 'common sense', on the astral and mental planes. 'Common sense' is an eloquent testimony to the oneness of our indwelling lives: we see all things around us on the physical plane in the same way, because our apparently separate consciousnesses are all really part of the one consciousness ensouling all forms. We all respond in the same general way, according to the stage of our evolution, because we share the same consciousness; and we are affected similarly by the same things because the action and re-action between them and ourselves is the interplay of one life in varied forms.

Recovery of anything by memory, then, is due to the ever-existence of everything in the consciousness of the LOGOS, and He has imposed upon us the limitations of time and space in order that we may, by pratice, be able to respond swiftly by changes of consciousness to the vibrations caused in our vehicles by vibrations coming from other vehicles similarly ensouled by consciousness; thus only can we gradually learn to distinguish precisely and clearly; contacting things successively — that is, being in time — and contacting them in relative directions in regard to ourselves and to each other — that is, being in space — we are gradually unfolded to the state in which we can recognize all simultaneously and each everywhere — that is, out of time and space.

As we pass through countless happenings in life we find that we do not keep in touch with all through which we have passed; there is a very limited power of response in our physical vehicle, and hence numerous experiences drop out of its purview. In trance, we can recover these, and they are said to emerge from the sub-conscious. Truly they remain ever unchanging in the universal Consciousness, and as we pass by them we become aware of them, because the very limited light of our consciousness, shrouded in the physical vehicle, falls upon them, and they disappear as we pass on; but as the area covered by that same light shining through the astral vehicle is larger, they again appear when we are in trance — that is in the astral vehicle, free from the physical; they have not come and gone and come back again, but the light of our consciousness in the physical vehicle had passed on and so we saw them not, and the more extended light in the astral vehicle enables us to see them again. As Bhagavan Das has well said:

'If a spectator wandered unrestingly through the halls of a vast museum, a great art gallery, at the dead of night, with a single small lamp in one hand, each of the natural objects, the pictured scenes, the statues, the portraits, would be illumined by that lamp, in succession, for a single moment, while all the rest were in darkness, and after that single moment, would itself fall into darkness again. Let there now be not one but countless such spectators, as many in endless number as the objects of sight within the place, each spectator meandering in and out incessantly through the great crowd of all the others, each lamp bringing momentarily into light one object and for only that spectator who holds that lamp. This immense and unmoving building is the rock-bound ideation of the changeless Absolute. Each lamp- carrying spectator out of the countelss crowd is one line of consciousness out of the pseudo-infinite lines of such that make up the totality of the one universal consciousness. Each coming into light of each object is it patency, is an experience of the jiva; each falling into darkness in its lapse into the latent. From the standpoint of the objects themselves, or of the universal consciousness, there is no latency, nor patency. From that of the lines of consciousness, there is'. [*The Science of Peace*, second edition, pp. 341-342]

## Consciousness 'Turns its Attention'

As vehicle after vehicle comes to fuller working, the area of light extends, and the consciousness can turn its attention to any one part of the area and observe closely the objects therein included. Thus, when the consciousness can function freely on the astral plane, and is aware of its surroundings there, it can see much that on the physical plane is 'past' — or 'future', if they be things to which in the 'past' it has learned to respond. Things outside the area of light coming through the vehicle of the astral body will be within the area of that which streams from the subtler mental vehicle. When the causal body is the vehicle, the 'memory of past lives' is recoverable, the causal body vibrating more readily to events to which it has before vibrated, and the light shining through it embracing a far larger area and illuminating scenes long 'past' — those scenes being really no more past than the scenes of the present, but occupying a different spot in time and space. The lower vehicles, which have not previously vibrated to these events, cannot readily directly contact them and answer to them; that belongs to the causal body, the relatively permanent vehicle. But when this body answers to them, the vibrations from it readily run downwards, and may be reproduced in the mental, astral and physical bodies.

The phrase is used above, as to consciousness, that 'it can turn its attention to any one part of the area, and observe closely the objects therein included'. This 'turning of the attention' corresponds very closely in consciousness to what we should call focusing the eye in the physical body. If we watch the action taking place in the muscles of the eye when we look first at a near and then at a distant object, or vice versa, we shall be conscious of a slight movement, and this constriction or relaxation causes a slight compression or the reverse in the lenses of the eye. It is an automatic action now, quite instinctive, but it has only become so by practice; a baby does not focus his eye, nor judge distance. He grasps as readily at a candle on the other side of the room as at one within his reach, and only slowly learns to know what is beyond his reach. The effort to see clearly leads to the focusing of the eye, and presently it becomes automatic. The objects for which the eye is focused are within the field of clear vision, and the rest are vaguely seen. So, also, the consciousness is clearly aware of that to which its attention is turned; other things remain vague, 'out of focus'.

A man gradually learns thus to turn his attention to things long past, as we measure time. The causal body is put into touch with them, and the vibrations are then transmitted to the lower bodies. The presence of a more advanced student will help a less advanced, because when the astral body of the former has been made to vibrate responsively to long past events, thus creating an astral picture of them, the astral body of the younger student can more readily reproduce these vibrations and thus also 'see'. But even when a man has learned to put himself into touch with his past, and through, his own with that of others connected with it, he will find it more difficult to turn his attention effectively to scenes with which he has had no connection; and when that is mastered, he will still find it difficult to put himself into touch with scenes outside the experiences of his recent past; for instance, if he wishes to visit the moon, and by his accustomed methods launches himself in that direction, he will find himself bombarded by a hail of unaccustomed vibrations to which he cannot respond, and will need to fall back on his inherent divine power to answer to anything which can affect his vehicles. If he seeks to go yet further, to another planetary chain, he will find a barrier he cannot overleap, the Ring Pass-not of his own planetary Logos.

We thus begin to understand what is meant by the statements that people at a certain grade of evolution can reach this or that part of the cosmos; they can put themselves into touch with the consciousness of the LOGOS outside the limitations imposed by their material vehicles on the less evolved. These vehicles, being composed of matter modified by the action of the planetary Logos of the chain to which they belong, cannot respond to the vibrations of matter differently modified; and the student must be able to use his Atmic body before he can contact the universal memory beyond the limits of his own chain.

Such is the theory of memory which I present for the consideration of theosophcal students. It applies equally to the small memories and forgettings of everyday life as to the vast reaches alluded to in the above paragraphs. For there is nothing small or great to the LOGOS, and when we are performing the smallest act of memory, we are as much putting ourselves into touch with the omnipresence and omniscience of the LOGOS, as when we are recalling a far-off past. There is no 'far- off, and no 'near'. All are equally present at all times and in all spaces; the difficulty is with our vehicles, and not with that all- embracing changeless life. All becomes more and more intelligible and more peace-giving as we think of that Consciousness, in which is no 'before' and no 'after', no 'past' and no 'future'. We begin to feel that these things are but the illusion, the limitations, imposed upon us by our own sheaths, necessary until our powers are evolved and at our service. We live unconsciously in this mighty Consciousness in which everything is eternally present, and we dimly feel that if we could live consciously in that Eternal there were peace. I know of nothing that can more give to the events of life their true proportion than this idea of a Consciousness in which everything is present from the beginning, in which indeed there is no beginning and no ending. We learn that there is nothing terrible and nothing which is more than relatively sorrowful; and in that lesson is the beginning of a true peace, which in due course shall brighten into joy.

# MEMORY IN THE DYING

by H. P. Blavatsky

We find in a very old letter from a MASTER, written years ago to a member of the Theosophical Society, the following suggestive lines of the mental state of a dying man:

'At the last moment, the whole life is reflected in our memory and emerges from all the forgotten nooks and corners, picture after picture, one event after the other. The dying brain dislodges memory with a strong, supreme impulse; and memory restores faithfully every impression that has been entrusted to it during the period of the brain's activity. That impression and thought which was the strongest, naturally becomes the most vivid, and survives, so to say, all the rest, which now vanish and disappear forever, to reappear but in Devachan. No man dies insane or unconscious, as some physiologists assert. Even a madman or one in a fit of *derilium tremens* will have his instant of perfect lucidity at the moment of death, though unable to say so to those present. The man may often appear dead. Yet from the last pulsation, from and between the last throbbing of his heart and the moment when the last spark of animal heat leaves the body, *the brain thinks* and the *Ego* lives over in those few brief seconds, his whole life over again. Speak in whispers, ye who assist at a deathbed and find yourselves in the solemn presence of Death. Especially have you to keep quiet just after Death has laid her clammy hand upon the body. Speak in whispers I say, lest you disturb the quiet ripple of thought and hinder the busy work of the Past casting its reflection upon the veil of the Future. . . . [*The Mahatma Letters to A P Sinnett,* Theosophical Publishing House, Letter 93B, 1979, p 167]

The above statement has been more than once strenuously opposed by materialists; biology and [scientific] psychology, it was urged, were both against the idea, and while the latter had no well demonstrated data to go upon in such a *hypothesis*, the former dismissed the idea as an empty 'superstition'. Meanwhile, even biology is bound to progress, and this is what we learn of its latest achievements. Dr Ferré) has communicated quite recently to the Biological Society of Paris a very curious note on the mental state of the dying, which corroborates marvellously the above lines. For, it is to the special phenomenon of life-reminiscences, and that sudden re-emerging on the blank walls of memory, from all its long neglected and forgotten 'nooks and corners', of 'picture after picture' that Dr Ferré) draws the special attention of biologists. [See recent researches of Dr Raymond Moody, Dr E Kubler Ross and others offer further confirmation]

We need notice but two among the numerous instances given by this scientist in his *Rapport*, to show how scientifically correct are the teachings we receive from our eastern Masters.

The first instance is that of a moribund consumptive whose disease was developed in consequence of a spinal affection. Already consciousness had left the man, when, recalled to life by two successive injections of a gram of ether, the patient slightly lifted his head and began talking rapidly in Flemish, a language no one around him, nor yet himself, understood. Offered a pencil and a piece of white cardboard, he wrote with great rapidity several lines in that language — very correctly, as was ascertained later on — fell back, and died. When translated —the writing was found to refer to a very prosaic affair. He had suddenly recollected, he wrote, that he owed a certain man a sum of fifteen francs since 1868 — hence more than twenty years — and desired it to be paid.

But why write his last wish in Flemish? The defunct was a native of Antwerp, but had left his country in childhood, without ever knowing the language, and having passed all his life in Paris, could speak and write only in French. Evidently his returning consciousness, that last flash of memory that displayed before him, as in a retrospective panorama, all his life, even to the trifling fact of his having borrowed twenty years back a few francs from a friend, did not emanate from his *physical* brain alone, but rather from his spiritual memory, that of the *Higher Ego* [Manas or the reincarnating individuality]. The fact of his speaking and writing Flemish, a language that he had heard at a time of life when he could not yet speak himself, is an additional proof. The EGO *is almost omniscient in its immortal nature*. For indeed matter is nothing more than 'the last degree and as the shadow of existence', as Ravaisson, member of the French Institute, tells us.

But to our second case.

Another patient, dying of pulmonary consumption and likewise re-animated by an injection of ether, turned his head towards his wife and rapidly said to her: 'You cannot find that pin now; all the floor has been renewed since then'. This was in reference to the loss of a scarf pin eighteen years before, a fact so trifling that it had almost been forgotten, but which had not failed to be revived in the last thought of the dying man, who having expressed what he saw in words, suddenly stopped and breathed his last. Thus any one of the thousand little daily events, and accidents of a long life would seem capable of being recalled to the flickering consciousness, at the supreme moment of dissolution. A long life, perhaps, lived over again in the space of one short second!

## Somnambulistic Memory

A third case may be noticed, which corroborates still more strongly that assertion of occultism which traces all such remembrances to the thought-power of the *individual*, instead of to that of the personal lower self. A young girl, who had been a sleep-walker up to her twenty-second year, performed during her hours of somnambulistic sleep the most varied functions of domestic life, of which she had no remembrance upon awakening.

Among other psychic impulses that manifested themselves only during her sleep was a secretive tendency quite alien to her waking state. During the latter she was open and frank to a degree, and very careless of her personal property; but in the somnambulistic state she would take articles belonging to herself or within her reach and hide them away with ingenious cunning. This habit being known to her friends and relatives, and two nurses, having been in attendance to watch her actions during her night rambles for years, nothing disappeared but what could be easily restored to its usual place. But on one sultry night, the nurse falling asleep, the young girl got up and went to her father's study. The latter, a notary of fame, had been working till a late hour that night. It was during a momentary absence from his room that the somnambulist entered, and deliberately possessed herself of a will left open upon the desk, as also of sum of several thousand pounds in bonds and notes. These she proceeded to hide in the hollow of two dummy pillars set up in the library to match the solid ones, and stealing from the room before her father's return, she regained her chamber and bed without awakening the nurse who was still asleep in the armchair.

The result was that, as the nurse stoutly denied that her young mistress had left the room, suspicion was diverted from the real culprit and the money could not be recovered. The loss of the will involved a lawsuit which almost beggared her father and entirely ruined his reputation, and the family were reduced to great straits. About nine years later the young girl who, during the previous seven years had not been somnambulistic, fell into a consumption of which she ultimately died. Upon her death-bed, the veil which had hung before her physical memory was raised; her divine insight awakened; the pictures of her life came streaming back before her inner eye; and among others she saw the scene of her somnambulistic robbery. Suddenly arousing herself from the lethargy in which she had lain for several hours, her face showed signs of some terrible emotion working within, and she cried out 'Ah! what have I done? ... It was I who took the will and the money. . . . Go search the dummy pillars in the library, I have . . .' She never finished her sentence for her very emotion killed her. But the search was made and the will and money found within the oaken pillars as she had said. What makes the case more strange is, that these pillars were so high, that even by standing upon a chair and with plenty of time at her disposal instead of only a few moments, the somnambulist could not have reached up and dropped the objects into the hollow columns. It is to be noted, however, that ecstatics and convulsionists (*Vide the Convulsionnaires de St Médard et de Morzīne*) seem to possess an abnormal facility for climbing blank walls and leaping even to the tops of trees.

## Brain Canal between Two Planes

Taking the facts as stated, would they not induce one to believe that the somnambulistic personage possesses an intelligence and memory of its own apart from the physical memory of the waking lower self; and that it is the former which remembers in *articulo mortis*, the body and physical senses in the latter case ceasing to function, and the intelligence gradually making its final escape through the avenue of psychic and, last of all, of spiritual conciousness? And why not? Even materialistic science begins now to concede to psychology more than one fact that would have vainly begged of it recognition twenty years ago. 'The real existence' Ravaisson tells us, 'the life of which every other life is but an imperfect outline, a faint sketch, is that of the Soul'. That which the public in general calls 'soul', we speak of as the 'reincarnating Ego'. 'To be, is to live, and to live is to will and think', says the French scientist. [*Rapport sur la Philosophie en France au XIXme Siècle.*] But, if indeed the physical brain is of only a limited area, the field for the containment of rapid flashes of unlimited and infinite thought, neither will nor thought can be said to be generated *within* it, even according to materialistic science, the impassable chasm between matter and mind having been confessed both by Tyndall and many others. The fact is that the human brain is simply the canal between two planes — the psycho-spiritual and the material —through which every abstract and metaphysical idea filters from the Manasic down to the lower human consciousness. Therefore, the ideas about the infinite and the absolute are not, nor can they be, within *our* brain capacities. They can be faithfully mirrored only by our spiritual consciousness, thence to be more or less faintly projected on to the tables of our perceptions on this plane. Thus while the records of even important events are often obliterated from our memory, not the most trifling action of our lives can disappear from the 'soul's' memory, because it is no MEMORY for it, but an ever present reality on the plane which lies outside our conceptions of space and time. 'Man is the measure of all things', said Aristotle; and surely he did not mean by man, the form of flesh, bones and muscles!

## In Us Rests the Unreachable

Of all the deep thinkers Edgard Quinet, the author of *Creation*, expressed this idea the best. Speaking of man, full of feelings and thoughts of which he has either no consciousness at all, or which he feels only as dim and hazy impressions, he shows that man realizes quite a small portion only of his moral being. 'The thoughts we think, but are unable to define and formulate, once repelled, seek refuge in the very root of our being. . . .' When chased by the persistent efforts of our will 'they retreat before it, still further, still deeper into — who knows what — fibres, but wherein they remain to reign and impress us unbidden and unknown to ourselves. . . .'

Yes; they become as imperceptible and as unreachable as the vibrations of sound and colour when these surpass the normal range. Unseen and eluding grasp, they yet work, and thus lay the foundations of our future actions and thoughts, and obtain mastery over us, though we may never think of them and are often ignorant of their very being and presence. Nowhere does Quinet, the great student of nature, seem more right in his observations than when speaking of the mysteries with which we are all surrounded: 'The mysteries of neither earth nor heaven but those present in the marrow of our bones, in our brain cells, our nerves and fibres. 'No need', he adds, 'in order to search for the unknown, to lose ourselves in the realm of the stars, when here, near us and *in us*, rests the unreachable. As our world is mostly formed of imperceptible beings which are the real constructors of its continents, so likewise is man'.

Verily so; since man is a bundle of obscure, and to himself unconscious perceptions, of indefinite feelings and misunderstood emotions, of ever forgotten memories and knowledge that becomes on the surface of his plane — *ignorance*. Yet, while physical memory in a healthy living man is often obscured, one fact crowding out another weaker one, at the moment of the great change that men call death — that which we call 'memory' seems to return to us in all its vigour and freshness.

May this not be due as just said, simply to the fact that, for a few seconds at least, our two memories [or rather the two states, the highest and the lowest states of consciousness] blend together, thus forming one, and that the dying being finds himself on a plane wherein there is neither past nor future, but all is one present? Memory, as we all know, is strongest with regard to its early associations, then when the future man is only a child, and more of a soul than of a body and if memory is a part of our soul, then, as Thackeray has somewhere said, it must be of necessity eternal. Scientists deny this; we, theosophists, affirm that it is so. They have for what they hold but negative proofs; we have, to support us, innumerable facts of the kind just instanced, in the three cases described by us. The links of the chain of cause and effect with relation to mind are, and must ever remain a *terra-incognita* to the materialist. For if they have already acquired a deep conviction that as Pope says:

Lulled in the countless chambers of the brain
Our thoughts are linked by many a *hidden* chain ...

— and that they are still unable to discover these chains, how can they hope to unravel the mysteries of the higher, spiritual, mind?

H.P.B.

www.ingramcontent.com/pod-product-compliance
Lightning Source LLC
LaVergne TN
LVHW041500070426
835507LV00009B/708